The Dodo Experiment

Martin Travers and Chloe Wyper

T0228716

methuen | drama

LONDON • NEW YORK • OXFORD • NEW DELHI • SYDNEY

METHUEN DRAMA
Bloomsbury Publishing Plc
50 Bedford Square, London, WC1B 3DP, UK
1385 Broadway, New York, NY 10018, USA
29 Earlsfort Terrace, Dublin 2, Ireland

BLOOMSBURY, METHUEN DRAMA and the Methuen
Drama logo are trademarks of Bloomsbury Publishing Plc

First published in Great Britain 2022

Cover photography: Alistair Devine

Cover image design: Jason Brown, Greenlight Creative

A catalogue record for this book is available from the British Library.

Library of Congress Control Number: 2022933990

ISBN: PB: 978-1-3503-4023-7
ePDF: 978-1-3503-4024-4
eBook: 978-1-3503-4025-1

Series: Modern Plays

Typeset by Mark Heslington Ltd, Scarborough, North Yorkshire

To find out more about our authors and books visit
www.bloomsbury.com and sign up for our newsletters.

The Dodo Experiment was first presented by the Citizens Theatre in a purpose-built temporary theatre space in Princes House, West Campbell Street, Glasgow, on 20 April 2022. The original cast in order of appearance was as follows:

Maddie Douglas/Parlour-Maid/ Freddy Eynsford-Hill	**Louise Scott**
Layla Arnoult/Mrs Eynsford-Hill	**Shannon Lynch**
David Knoh/Henry Higgins	**Allan Othieno**
Peggy Mackay/Miss Eliza Doolittle	**Natalie Rochacelli**
Aria Reilly/Miss Clara Eynsford-Hill	**Genna Allan**
Bella Constantine/Mrs Higgins	**Caitlin Ruby Muir**
Hugo Winston/Colonel Pickering	**Hunter Christian Jessen**
Marcus Oates/Trevor Rivers	**Kieran McKenzie**
Director/Tannoy	**Erin McAuley** (Voice)

Director	Fiona Mackinnon
Set Designer	Christine Ting-Huan 挺歡 Urquhart
Costume Designer	Elaine Coyle
Lighting Designer	Stuart Jenkins
Composer/Sound Designer	Calum Paterson
Fight Director	EmmaClaire Brightlyn
Choreographer/Movement	Daniel Brawley

THANKS

Clare Macaulay, Carly McCaig, Maureen Carr, Megan Kay, Sarah Mcadam and all the wonderful Citizens Theatre staff for their support throughout the project and final production.

SPECIAL THANKS

Arts in the City, Glasgow Life, Glasgow City Council Social Work Services, Creative Scotland, The National Lottery and the Life Changes Trust.

CITIZENS THEATRE

The Citizens Theatre is Glasgow's major producing theatre and one of the leading theatre companies in the UK. Over the last 75 years, the Citizens has built an international reputation for producing innovative shows on stage, alongside a highly regarded learning programme of participatory and education work. Fondly known as the Citz, the company presents bold new interpretations of classic texts and, uniquely, allows any member of the audience to attend a performance for as little as 50p.

The Citizens Learning Team has an international reputation for excellence in its field, and in a typical year delivers over 50 projects. The team's activity includes drama classes for children and adults and all ages and abilities throughout the year and projects with care-experienced young adults; offenders in prison communities, and ex-offenders and their families; vulnerable women, either in a residential care setting or who are experiencing homelessness; people who are in recovery and/or have been through or have experience of the criminal justice system; children with emotional and behavioural difficulties, and asylum seekers and refugees.

For the latest information about the Citizens Theatre visit citz.co.uk

It was 2002 when I first stepped into a Glasgow social work office to take up the newly created role of Arts Development Worker. Thanks to the foresight of some forward-thinking individuals who understood the power of the arts to enrich and transform lives, the post was the first dedicated arts development role within social work in the city. It was designed to encourage young people aged between sixteen and twenty-six with experience of being in care into the creative arts. Naturally at first there was some scepticism from staff who would rather have had additional social workers to manage the growing caseloads and viewed the arts as merely a pastime, a distraction rather than a real tool for change.

In contrast to the luxury of the theatre company where I had been previously employed, there were times when it felt like I'd walked into the set of a police crime drama on television. There were phones ringing off the hook, people rushing around responding to urgent calls for assistance and young people presenting with pressing problems. My confidence wavered – had we overestimated how the arts could help?

Initially the plan was for a one-year programme offering high-quality drama. photography and film-making workshops. Young care leavers helped design the programme. With their help we recognised the need for flexibility and a holistic approach that provided fares and meals and most importantly professional artists. Artists who not only were amongst the best in their chosen field but had a real desire to create safe, inclusive atmospheres where young people could flourish. If the programme could demonstrate a positive impact on young people, there was hope it could continue.

And continue it did. An ever-expanding programme of art activities was introduced – music, visual art and dance to name a few. Then the programme was extended to cater for all ages from nought to twenty-six. In addition to the participatory workshops, young people presented multi-media performances in Glasgow theatres, displayed art works in prominent galleries and attended a diverse programme of performances.

The project, which young people named 'Arts in the City', proved itself to be an asset and valuable tool within social work. An external evaluation in the early years of the project reported that 'the testimony of young people and of those who worked with them provides ample evidence that the programme of activity had a positive impact on their self-confidence, group and communications skills … It's given people a chance to experience new things, meet each other and help build relationships, confidences and self-esteem.'

The 'Arts in the City' programme continues to expand and deliver innovative creative opportunities for young care-experienced people to this day. Having initially proved the worth of participatory artistic engagement it was important to continue to find sustainable long-term opportunities for future generations of care-experienced young people.

In March 2017 I was invited by Professor Louise Hill, who was at the time working for the Centre for Excellence for Children's Care and Protection, to join a steering group to help build, develop and empower a unique theatre ensemble for the many diverse and talented care-experienced young people within Glasgow and the surrounding area. Along with Carly McCaig, Martin Travers and Guy Hollands from the Citizens Theatre we developed the original idea into a detailed plan and the first seeds of the wonderful WAC Ensemble were sown.

We were all delighted when the Life Changes Trust funded this initial period of development, recruitment and delivery for the project.

A lot of thought and preparation went into making the conditions right for these young theatre-makers to engage and learn, but the real success of the WAC Ensemble is down to the amazing young people who brought their energy and dedication to every session. Their shared experiences nurtured trust and bonding from the start, and they quickly became a focussed team. They embraced their love of theatre along with the opportunity to re-write the preconceived ideas held by many of the public towards young people with care experience.

With support from Creative Scotland the company continued to flourish. The WAC Ensemble are actors first and foremost and now have a plethora of credits, including four-star reviews from theatre critics and sold-out performances of *Whatever Happened to the Jaggy Nettles?* This was their first full production; as well as winning high and lasting praise from the public, in February 2022 it was the proud recipient of the Writers' Guild Best New Play for Young Audiences.

Their other work includes leading workshops with other care-experienced young people, festival appearances and professional engagements with other theatre companies. Even Covid didn't stop them. When live performance wasn't an option, they created the heart-warming Christmas show *Elf Strike!* on Zoom in December 2020, while working remotely to create the dark and slightly terrifying radio play *Cupid, Draw Back Your Bow* in the spring and summer of 2021.

Their current production *The Dodo Experiment*, co-written by Martin Travers and WAC Ensemble founding member Chloe Wyper, is their most ambitious project yet. Here's hoping we can continue to secure funding for the future of this unique ensemble. It feels like they've changed the link between care experience and theatre-making in Scotland for ever ... and they've only just started their journey!

Clare Macaulay, Arts Development Worker
Arts in the City, Glasgow Health and Social Care Partnership

As I write this, we are about a quarter of the way through rehearsals and have just reached the 'playing with stuff on its feet' phase. This is an exciting point in the process where the characters and the world start to come to life. *The Dodo Experiment* is an action-packed, post-Covid nightmare that blends a scary contemporary world with classical text. There is so much for the actors and me to explore and it's been great having Martin in the room while we do table work. Martin brings so much detail and openness when responding to questions or notes, as well as an uplifting energy that never falters. Chloe Wyper hasn't been in the room as much (she gave birth to her wee baby just before we started rehearsals!) but she has still been very much involved in the rehearsals, responding through emails and Zoom calls. This is Chloe's first full-length play, yet she writes dialogue with ease, has confidence in her choices and knows her characters and world inside out. She's a powerhouse.

One of the magic things about new writing is that you are the first people to imagine what this world might be like. The characters in the play are rehearsing George Bernard Shaw's *Pygmalion,* but they themselves are in this vivid and dangerous world within *The Dodo Experiment,* so it's a world within a world. As well as that, this show will premiere at the Princes House, an abandoned office block in Glasgow, so it's a really exciting design challenge for myself and the creative and production teams. There's the opportunity to play with the audience's sense of reality from the moment they arrive at the location of the show. I have been working closely with Christine Ting-Huan 挺歡 Urquhart, set and prop designer on the show, who is ambitious and detail driven, making sure that the *Pygmalion* set and the mayhem that has already happened as part of the 'experiment' is represented within the space. We are still at the initial design phase of the process as I write this, but I have really valued the collaboration with Christine. The audience are in for a unique experience from the moment they walk up to the Princes House building.

The Dodo Experiment highlights how exploitative the theatre industry can be, particularly for young actors. The play is an exaggerated scenario, but it's rooted in an unfortunate reality. A shortage of jobs and lack of funding mean actors are too often expected to feel grateful for work despite bad conditions and/or unsafe practice. As a company of young actors, the WAC Ensemble were keen to highlight and explore this issue in this story. Drama school training is expensive (the audition fee alone is costly!), so programmes like WAC make training more accessible and attempt to address this imbalance. Most of the ensemble are juggling jobs, studies, families and other life stuff on top of their rehearsals, so the team at the Citizens make the schedule work around the performers' other commitments. This collaboration and commitment from all involved is the reason that it works. The WAC Ensemble are a passionate, talented group of performers and artists, and I feel lucky to have the opportunity to work with them. A pioneering attitude to change, a vibrant curiosity in all people, weird and brilliant minds, and a readiness to challenge the old ways of doing things will keep the industry burning bright. I can't wait until WAC are running theatres.

With that all being said, I better get back to rehearsals …

Fiona Mackinnon
Director of *The Dodo Experiment*

Since 2018, I have been a member of the Citizens Theatre's WAC Ensemble. During those four years, I have raised my confidence as a performer and now as an emerging playwright. In 2021, I tried something new. I put my writing skills into practice. I was unable to act in the upcoming company production because I was going to have a baby, so I was given the opportunity to co-write *The Dodo Experiment* with Martin Travers. I have written poems, short plays and stories in the past but having the opportunity to do something this in-depth and getting the experience to work with someone as experienced as Martin was really an honour for me.

Working on the script for this project really pushed me out of my comfort zone. I am used to being the one onstage performing the material but this time I was the one behind the scenes providing it, which was really nerve wracking but really exciting for me. I loved working with the WAC Ensemble, using their improvisations to get into the heads of the characters in the play and understand the world of this dark experiment in a way I never thought I could have before.

A big highlight was getting to work with director and actor Maureen Carr during our script development phase. I've admired Maureen's work for years so to be able to work with her, having conversations about this imaginary world and the story we were building was really special for me. It was so interesting, and I learned a lot from her insight into how best to nurture new writing.

I'm really proud of my work on *The Dodo Experiment*. The support and encouragement I've been getting from Martin and Maureen has inspired me to continue writing. I've learned a lot about myself as a writer and I'm starting to believe that there is more to me than solely being an actor. I now know I can do whatever I put my mind to. *The Dodo Experiment* is my first full-length play, but it won't be my last. So watch this space!

Chloe Wyper

I was delighted when playwright Martin Travers asked me to be involved with the Citizens Theatre's WAC Ensemble intensive script development for *The Dodo Experiment*. It was amazing watching the play evolve over the ten weeks. Working with this talented group of young actors has been so exciting and I've learned so much from them. It really was a team effort; everyone involved had a voice and felt safe in giving their opinions.

It was especially exciting to see Chloe Wyper's confidence grow every week in her writing abilities, with support and guidance from Martin. They are in excellent hands with Fiona Mackinnon as director of the production. I wish them all the best and look forward to seeing *The Dodo Experiment* being brought to life.

Maureen Carr

I can't believe I've known some of the WAC ensemble for four years now. To be allowed the chance to watch young actors improve their skills and hone their talents over such a long period of time has been a revelation. I genuinely believe that there's nothing this gang of theatre makers can't do if they set their minds to it.

Last summer WAC member and emerging writer Chloe Wyper told me she wouldn't be able to be in our new, still-to-be-written, play because she was going to have a baby. Straight away I asked her if she wanted to co-write the play with me. Chloe's a direct writer. Clever. No flimflam. Her dialogue is funny and tight. To get to work with her closely on *The Dodo Experiment* has been a ball. And for her to sign off on the first draft of the play just days before she gave birth to her wee girl is the stuff of legend.

We were really lucky to have the support of director and actor Maureen Carr during our script development phase in autumn 2021. Although we were at that point able to meet in a room with the full WAC Ensemble to improvise and test out story ideas, these sessions were always challenging due to the ever-present threat of Covid-19, people isolating, social distancing and the constant mask wearing. During these sessions Maureen's energy and unceasing confidence in the play we were building never wavered.

I suppose it is worth saying a wee bit about what inspired this weird and at points brutal play. In the summer of 2021, ensemble member Genna Allan had suggested that we write a play about actors in a rehearsal room. Then ensemble member Allan Othieno added that he wanted the play to be contemporary or set in the near future. These two strong ideas were the starting point of our journey together to create *The Dodo Experiment*. We also knew that the extract of the play we wanted the characters to be rehearsing in the story had to be from a classic play. When we found out – to our delight – that the works of George Bernard Shaw had come into the public domain in 2021 we quickly settled on the scene being from *Pygmalion*. Once we had that piece of the jigsaw, there was no holding us back.

Having the opportunity to bring in the fantastically talented Fiona Mackinnon to direct the play has really galvanised the ensemble. I can't wait to see the production in April 2022. I know it is going to be a vicious and theatrical delight.

Martin Travers
Playwright

The Dodo Experiment

*MT: Dedicated to Jane and Mary Ellen
and all our magnolia memories*

CW: Dedicated to my daughter Aimee-Ross Halliday

Characters

David Knoh/Henry Higgins
Bella Constantine/Mrs Higgins
Maddie Douglas/Parlour-Maid/Freddy Eynsford-Hill
Hugo Winston/Colonel Pickering
Layla Arnoult/Mrs Eynsford-Hill
Aria Reilly/Miss Clara Eynsford-Hill
Peggy Mackay/Miss Eliza Doolittle
Marcus Oates/Trevor Rivers
Tannoy: Pre-Recorded Voice
Director: Pre-Recorded Voice

All direct instructions that come through the **Tannoy** system are delivered by the same voice in a creepy yet polite received pronunciation.

Writers' Note: In this version of the play **Maddie** is Scottish. She doesn't need to be Scottish in other productions, but she does need to be an outsider from another country (or region).

Set

An ominous and stark room in an abandoned warehouse. A **Tannoy** system and security cameras show that the room is under constant observation. The room is set up like a rehearsal room – costume rails, mirrors, make-up, general actor-generated detritus. Some broken furniture and other visible damage show signs of a previous outburst of mass rage. One part of the room is set up as **Mrs Higgins'** drawing room in *Pygmalion*. One part of the set has a dining table and chairs with beautiful place settings and candelabras, but the tablecloth is badly stained by four months of the group eating there. Crates and/or plain cardboard boxes of gin are piled up against a wall. One door at the back of the stage leads to the sleeping area – a sign above the door reads 'You Shall Sleep in a Proper Bedroom'. Another door leads to an area marked 'Incinerator Room'. There are two chairs in the corner of the room facing each other – on one of the chairs there's a pile of wires and dismantled components that **Hugo** is using to try to build a makeshift radio.

Costume

The characters wear their *Pygmalion* costumes throughout the play. They have been wearing these costumes constantly for four months. Some of their clothing might be understandably damaged or stained. They are not given any water to wash with, so their hair and completions are grubby and oily. When **Trevor** appears, he's dressed in black – t-shirt, modern military-style combat trousers, combat jacket and heavy boots.

Scene One

Good Is Not Good Enough

*Day one. We hear the whirr of the security cameras and some light feedback coming from the **Tannoy** system. The room is in darkness. As the lights slowly fade up **Maddie** and **Layla** hurry into the room from the sleeping area offstage. They are putting on the last part of their costumes – probably their hats. They look tired and ill – like forgotten hostages. **Layla** tries to stay in character as **Mrs Eynsford-Hill** throughout most of the play but this mask slips occasionally when she is losing her temper.*

Maddie A couldnae sleep last night. Acause ae aw yer snorin.

Layla You must be mistaken. A lady does not snore!

Maddie So A did some sums.

Layla How delightfully charming.

Maddie Whit is? Yer snorin? Nothin charmin aboot this.

*She pretends to snore like a bull. **Layla** grabs **Maddie**'s face with one hand – **Maddie** stops pretending to snore and looks scared. **Layla** puts on a massive fake grin before she lets **Maddie**'s face go.*

Layla Delighted to hear you have been practising your arithmetic. Self-improvement is why we are all here after all.

Maddie Aye – well. A dinnae feel self-improved. A feel hungry an tired an sick wi anxiety aw the time.

Layla You should learn to appreciate what they have given us. The director will come back. She said she would. In the meantime – we go through the motions. Work our fingers to the bone so to speak. This experiment is exactly what my career was crying out for.

Maddie No much ae a career so faur then, eh?

Layla *draws **Maddie** a dirty look.*

Maddie   When we finally perform the play we aw git ten grand each. Right?

Layla   Yes. To my knowledge. That's what it says in our contracts.

Maddie   Aye – well. We've been in this damp dump fir four months. Ten grand dividit bi four months. That's less than minimum wage! An we're no even hauf-wey throu finishin the script.

Layla (*being contrary*)   I didn't become an actor for the money.

Maddie   Ye wantin some long straw?

Layla   Why would I want long straw?

Maddie   Tae feed yer high horse!

Layla   I'm not in the mood to take your vulgar bait. (*Politely threatening her.*) I find conflict tiresome and can lead to terrible acts of violence. Go stand somewhere else. Somewhere over there. You smell.

Maddie   Whit? An you dinnae?

Layla   Petulant guttersnipe!

Maddie   Whit even is a guttersnipe?

Layla   You Maddie – are the very definition of a guttersnipe.

Maddie   A hope you're the next tae disappear.

Layla (*getting angry*)   They left!

Maddie   Aye – oot the blue in the middle ae the night efter trashin the place? (*Whispers.*) Bet ye thay're fried breid! How cin we finish *Pygmalion* wi'oot a Mrs Pearce? Or a Freddy? Or a Alfred P. feckin-Doolittle?

Layla   We'll double up all three parts if it comes to it!

Maddie Double up?! We keep disappearin at this rate an oor *Pygmalion*'ll end up bein a monologue! That incinerator's thare fir a reason. Juist sayin.

Layla *moves away from* **Maddie**. *Half asleep and led by* **David**, *the rest of the cast scurry in.* **David** *looks at his pocket watch.*

David 4.59 a.m. Quickly! Quickly! We want to do well today. The rules!

They all stand formally with their hands on their hearts as they melodramatically recite the rules of the experiment.

Peggy Actions have consequences

All until the end.

Aria We must know our place

All until the end.

Layla We must stay in character

All Until the end.

Bella We must improve

All until the end.

David We must suffer for our art

All and by doing so we will bloom!

The group stretch and shake – warming up. **Peggy** *goes up to* **Layla** *in needy actor mode.*

Peggy Layla. Sorry. Know it is rather early. Was just wondering. I've been thinking about Eliza's predicament. She's expected to improve but also to know her place. Like we are here. I'm finding that juxtaposition confusing. Any thoughts?

Layla (*delighted to be asked*) Oh not at all, Peggy. That's a very interesting /

Before she can finish her sentence **Bella** *interrupts her.*

Bella   / Why are you asking her that? She's not directing the play!

Peggy   Well – somebody has to.

Bella   Why don't you direct it?

Peggy   I'm not a director.

Bella   Exactly. And neither's she.

David   Places! Places, everybody!

Apart from **David**, **Peggy** *and* **Layla**, *they are lacklustre as they do a silly vocal warm-up before taking their places for a waltz. They yawn and sing half-heartedly as they waltz around the room with imaginary partners.*

All
    Come, come, come and make eyes at me
    Down at the Old Bull and Bush,
    Da, da, da, da, da,
    Come, come, drink some port wine with me,
    Down at the Old Bull and Bush,
    Hear the little German Band,
    Da, da, da, da, da,
    Just let me hold your hand dear,
    Do, do come and have a drink or two
    Down at the Old Bull and Bush.

The singing is interrupted by a blinding light.

Layla   STOP! STOP! You all need to try harder! Be better! Good just isn't good enough! See! See?! This what happens when all of you don't try a leg! We are here to /

She is cut off by a deafening and upsetting alarm and flashing lights.

The cast hunker down with their hands over their ears. Some of them let out stifled groans of pain.

Scene Two

The Auditions

Five months ago. The cast stand up one at a time and address the audience directly. Throughout the scene we only ever hear the cold and impatient voice of the **Director***. Each of the actors take a turn to step into the light. They are all now wearing disposable face masks. They take their masks off as they start their auditions apart from* **David** *who forgets. After they speak, they each take their places for the extract of* Pygmalion *they are rehearsing in the next scene.*

Peggy   Is live theatre dead? That's a really interesting question. Didn't expect that question. Eh. Hmmm. Eh. Not sure to be honest. Maybe it's run its course – so to speak. Hope not. No point in me being here if it was!

She laughs nervously and inappropriately.

I'm. I'm. I'm Peggy MacKay, reading for Eliza Doolittle.

She takes a deep breath.

Peggy (*as* **Eliza**)   There's menners f' yer!

She is having trouble with the pronunciation of the Cockney accent.

Te-oo banches o voy . . . voylets . . . trod into the mud. Ow, eez ye-ooa san, is e?

She stands in silence for five seconds that feels like ten minutes before breaking character.

Peggy   Can I start again? I do know it. I am prepared. I am professional – hard worker. It's just that London accent – not London – sorry – Cockney. It . . . can't get it to stick in my mouth. Hear it in my head, but it doesn't come out my lips. Sorry. Understand that my slot is only three minutes but please, I know this.

A light shines directly into her face. She loses her temper.

Will you stop shining that light in my face! I'm really good at what I do! Normally. Can I read for the Parlour-Maid instead? Please. I need this.

Bella *enters and is sick with nerves. She mumbles and stumbles her way through her audition.*

Bella   Hello, my name is Bella . . . (*She breathes out.*) Bella Constantine, and I'm reading for Mrs . . . er, Mrs Higgins. Sorry, two wee seconds, can't find my part. Really sorry.

She drops her script, and the pages get mixed up.

Oh – bloody-bloody-bloody-bloody bollocks!

She panics as she tries to get the sheets of paper back into order.

Eliza came to me this morning. She passed the night partly walking about . . . about in a rage, partly trying to throw herself into the river and . . . (*As herself.*) Oh, I forgot to do the bloody voice . . . Please, let me try again, I can do better. I'm not normally like this.

Bella (*as* **Mrs Higgins**)   Eliza came to me this . . . this morning.

She scans one of the mixed-up pages looking for her place but has jumped a section.

She passed the night partly walking about in a rage, partly . . .

She rips up the sheets of paper in a frenzy and throws them to the ground.

Bloody-bloody-bloody-bloody bollocks! I know that wasn't great, but I really have to do this part, this job.

Director   Who are you with?

Bella   Sorry. I'm not sure what /

Director   / What's your agent's name?

Bella (*serious*)   No. No. I don't have an agent – yet. Will that be an issue? Please! Seriously. Will it? I need this.

David *runs in, looking dishevelled and still tipsy from the night before.*

David   Sorry! Sorry – know I'm a tad late.

He is trying to hide his tiredness, but it is obvious that he is still under the influence. Throughout the scene, this is highlighted by grogginess and a slight slur of the words. He's also forgotten to take off his mask.

Sorry I'm late. Buses were a nightmare. And packed! If I don't have Covid after that I must be immune!

He is giggly through nerves as well as the alcohol sloshing about his system.

Okay. Who am I? Yes, I'm David Knoh, reading for the part of the Professor. Henry Higgins.

He reads straight from the script.

David (*as* **Higgins**)   I have never sneered in my life. Sneering doesn't become either the human face or the human soul. (*As himself.*) Pants! My mask.

He takes off his mask.

David (*as* **Higgins**)   I am expressing my righteous contempt for (*Struggling to read the word.*) *com-merc-i-al-ism.* I don't and won't trade in affection . . .

He burps loudly and immediately breaks character.

David (*giggling*)   Sorry about that. At least I never farted – eh? Better out than in though, right? Ooohft – wee whiff of curry sauce and chips there. (*To himself.*) Don't remember buying chips.

Director   Have you been drinking?

David (*inappropriately joking*)   At this time in the morning?! A'm not that bad yet. Was drinking last night though. Totally sloshed if I'm honest! Pie-eyed and guilty as charged. Ah, I've messed this up haven't I? Look, I'm not like this normally. You see, my girlfriend's pug died of heatstroke on Tuesday. Well, that and suffocation. How was I to know he'd went for a sleep in the tumble dryer? Know I should have checked before switching the machine on; but I'd had a few sherries. Wee idiot. Been couch surfing since. (*Lying.*) All good though! Then – you'll never believe it – got attacked by a mad swan last night. So went for a couple of cocktails. To calm my nerves. Sorry. Can you let me try again? Please? I need this.

Layla   Hi. I'm Layla Arnoult, reading for Mrs Eynsford Hill. Before I begin – just want to say that I'm so excited about this project. The Pygmalion Experiment sounds . . . well . . . pioneering. To live and breathe this play morning, noon and night for six months – I mean. The results will be fascinating! Ground-breaking. And I just adore George Bernard Shaw. His endless . . . I mean *epic* speeches haven't dated at all in my opinion. He really was a genius – don't you think? Oh – yes. My audition!

She fills the room with a hideously fake laugh. She takes a dramatic breath, puts her head down and raises it just before she begins her audition.

Layla (*as* **Mrs Eynsford-Hill**)   Oh, please, please, Clara. We should be so grateful to you, sir, if you found us a cab. Oh, thank you . . .

She stops acting.

Layla   I'm sorry but this just isn't working for me. I should be reading for Mrs Higgins, don't you think? I mean, it's a much bigger part. A better part. My talent would really go to waste as Mrs Eynsford-Hill. I'm being serious.

Director   We already have Mrs Higgins cast. This is more suitable for you.

Layla   More suitable?! How would you know?! I studied at
RADA. I have played Lady Macbeth. This old bat Eynsford-
Hill would really be a step down for me. Can I read for Mrs
Higgins?

*She looks out hopefully into the darkness, but she realises she is
getting nowhere.*

Okay! fine! I'll play Mrs Eynsford-Hill – as long as I get to
understudy Mrs Higgins. No, don't send me away. Please,
please. I need this.

Maddie   A'm Maddie Douglas. Here fir the part ae Mrs
Pearce?

She readies herself.

Maddie (*as* **Mrs Pearce**)   Will ye please keep tae the point,
Mr Higgins? A'm wantin tae ken on whit terms the girl is tae
be here. Is she tae hae ony wages? An whit is tae become ae
her whan ye've finisht yer teachin?! Yer needin tae leuk
aheid tae /

Director   / Do that again. But in English this time.

Maddie   Whit? Excuse me?! Yer wantin us tae pit on a
stupit accent? Eh, naw! A'm daen it ma ain wey! Ye git a
problem wi me? Ma actin?! Eh? Come doun here an say it
tae ma face. Ye 'hink ye're so great, sittin up thare pickin an
choosin. Ye know whit? Naebody'll be wantin tae come see
this crap onywey. (*Screams.*) Stick yer stupit ancient play up
yer great granny's gramophone!

She composes herself.

Maddie (*she smiles radiantly*)   Unless – that is – ye 'hink A'd
still be good fir it. Please? A'm needin this.

Hugo *picks his nose constantly through his audition.*

Hugo   Okay, will I just start? Great. (*As Macbeth and totally
over the top.*) Is this a dagger which I see before me? The
handle toward my hand? Come, let me clutch thee. I have

thee not, and yet I see thee still. Art thou not, fatal vision, sensible to feeling as to sight? Or art thou but a dagger of the mind /

Director   / Colonel Pickering. You are here to read for Colonel Pickering – from *Pygmalion*. George Bernard Shaw?

Hugo   Pygmy-what? To be honest, got some random Facebook message yesterday telling me about a dodgy acting job, some experiment – only scanned it. I do loads of extra work. Axes. Ginger beards. Feasting – drinking mead – that kinda shit. That's my thing. Not that I need the money – I'm totally minted. I'm a borderline tech genius. (*Beat.*) Will I get to wear a colonel's uniform? Medals and a sword? I've always wanted to act with an actual sword. Killing people on stage. All that fake blood. I've got a thing about knives.

Aria *comes in, obviously upset but tries to leave it at the door.*

Aria   Hi, I'm Aria Reilly, reading for Miss Eynsford-Hill, or Clara. I feel a real connection with Clara. Like me, she too is unlucky in love. Fated to drag her loneliness through her crushed life like a . . . heart-broken ball and chain.

Aria (*as* **Clara**)   If Freddy had a bit of gumption, he would have got one at the theatre door. Other people got cabs. Why couldn't he? Well, haven't you got a cab?

Her emotions get the best of her, and she bursts out crying.

Aria (*as herself*)   How could he do that to me?! I'm sorry. I'm just going through a really hard time right now. My world is ending. He was . . . *is* . . . my everything. I can change! I just need a chance! (*Composing herself.*) Should I continue? No?! Look, just got a bit emotional. I'll put him out my head. (*Cracking again.*) And my heart. Promise. Please. (*Shouts.*) I need this!

She drops to her knees and wails with heartbroken anguish.

Aria   Take me back, take me back, take me back!

Scene Three

Rehearsal Disrupted

Day one – later that afternoon. The cast quickly take their positions to rehearse. During their rehearsal **Trevor** *is heard climbing up a drainpipe and onto the roof. He is then heard walking over it. They are scared and distracted by the sounds coming from above them but try to focus and keep rehearsing*

Miss Eynsford-Hill (*flirting*)   I sympathize. I haven't any small talk. If people would only be frank and say what they really think!

Higgins (*gloomily*)   Lord forbid!

Mrs Eynsford-Hill   But why?

Higgins   What they think they ought to think is bad enough, Lord knows; but what they really think would break up the whole show. Do you suppose it would be really agreeable if I were to come out now with what I really think?

Miss Eynsford-Hill (*gaily*)   Is it so very cynical?

Higgins   Cynical! Who the dickens said it was cynical? I mean it wouldn't be decent.

Mrs Eynsford-Hill (*seriously*)   Oh! I'm sure you don't mean that, Mr Higgins.

Higgins   You see, we're all savages, more or less. We're supposed to be civilised and cultured – to know all about poetry and philosophy and art and science, and so on; but how many of us know even the meanings of these names? (*To* **Miss Eynsford-Hill**.) What do you know of poetry? What do you know of science? (*Indicating* **Freddy**.) What does he know of art or science or anything else? What the devil do you imagine I know of philosophy?

They hear heavy footsteps across the roof. This fills them with dread.

Mrs Higgins (*warningly*)   Or of manners, Henry?

The **Parlour-Maid** *speak as she opens the door.*

Parlour-Maid   Miss Doolittle.

The **Parlour-Maid** *withdraws.* **Higgins** *rises hastily and runs to* **Mrs Higgins**.

Higgins   Here she is, mother.

Liza (*speaking with pedantic correctness of pronunciation and great beauty of tone*)   How do you do, Mrs Higgins?

She gasps slightly in making sure of the H in Higgins but is quite successful.

Liza   Mr Higgins told me I might come.

Mrs Higgins (*cordially*)   Quite right: I'm very glad indeed to see you.

Pickering   How do you do, Miss Doolittle?

Liza (*shaking hands with him*)   Colonel Pickering, is it not?

Mrs Eynsford-Hill   I feel sure we have met before, Miss Doolittle. I remember your eyes.

Liza   How do you do?

Mrs Eynsford-Hill (*introducing*)   My daughter Clara.

Liza   How do you do?

Clara (*impulsively*)   How do you do?

Freddy   I've certainly had the pleasure.

Mrs Eynsford-Hill (*introducing*)   My son Freddy.

Liza   How do you do?

Freddy *bows and sits down, infatuated.*

Mrs Higgins   Henry, please!

Higgins *is about to sit on the edge of the table.*

Mrs Higgins   Don't sit on my writing-table: you'll break it.

Higgins (*sulkily*)   Sorry.

They all look up as the sounds from the roof are now directly above them. They look at each other in fear.

Mrs Higgins (*conversationally*)   Will it rain, do you think?

Liza   The shallow depression in the west of these islands is likely to move slowly in an easterly direction. There are no indications of any great change in the barometrical situation.

Freddy   Ha! ha! how awfully funny!

Liza   What is wrong with that, young man? I bet I got it right.

Freddy   Killing!

Mrs Eynsford-Hill   I'm sure I hope it won't turn cold. There's so much influenza about. It runs right through our whole family regularly every spring.

Liza (*darkly*)   My aunt died of influenza: so they said. But it's my belief they done the old woman in!

We hear two load bangs as **Trevor** *intentionally smashes through the skylight.* **Trevor** *drops through the skylight into the sleeping area. We hear another loud crack as the bed he lands on collapses. Everyone stops rehearsing. The lights in the room turn a sinister red and start to pulse slowly.*

Maddie   Whit the /

Hugo   / Did everybody hear that?

Bella   Of course we bloody heard it!

David   What's happening?!

Aria   Are we being punished again?

Tannoy   THERE HAS BEEN A SECURITY BREACH. LIE ON THE FLOOR WITH YOUR HANDS ON THE BACK OF YOUR HEADS.

Peggy   Don't you think that sounds like the director? Maybe it's her?

Layla   Don't be ridiculous.

Peggy   I'm sure it's her.

Everyone lies on their stomachs with their hands at the back of their heads. They are freaking out.

Aria   Stay calm!

Layla (*panicking*)   Yes. Everybody. Just. Just. Stay calm!

Peggy   Calm is not what I'm feeling! My body's telling me to run!

Trevor (*from sleeping quarters*)   Help! Help me! Think I've broken something. Can't move my back! Can't breathe. Help me!

Tannoy   DO NOT SPEAK TO THE INTRUDER. DO NOT GO TO THE AID OF THIS INTRUDER. LIE DOWN AND AWAIT NEW INSTRUCTIONS.

Maddie   Maybe he's part ae the experiment?

David   They're calling him an intruder!

Aria   They wouldn't call him that if he was part of this.

Hugo   That's what I was thinking.

Bella   He'll know where we are. He can tell us where we are.

Peggy   Maybe he's a new Alfred?

Maddie   A new Freddy?

Aria (*frustrated*)   He's just fell through the roof!

Tannoy   STAY ON THE FLOOR. AWAIT NEW INSTRUCTIONS.

Layla Aria's right. There is no way this, this, this *intrusion* is part of the experiment! Probably a drug addict. Or a pervert. Only drug addicts and perverts break lockdowns.

Bella We're in the middle of bloody nowhere. He's here for a reason.

Hugo Every time it rains my bed gets soaked. Maybe he's just here to fix the leaks in the roof?

Aria Well, he's not done a good job of it so far – has he?!

Bella He could be maintenance. Like the old man that used to come and empty the toilet bucket in the middle of the night. Before they took away our /

Aria (*mocking*)   / Maintenance? Don't be so stupid.

Peggy Maybe Hugo's right. There's black mould on my mattress too you know. Black mould can kill you. We should check he's okay. We might get new mattresses out of this. Fresh blankets at least! I would contemplate marrying a penniless octogenarian for a fresh feather pillow!

Aria Even if he is a worker – we should let *them* deal with him. The last thing we need is Covid in here.

David I'm with Aria. Layla?

Layla I agree. I think that we should . . . (*being melodramatic*) exercise caution!

Trevor Help me! PLEASE!

Maddie Sounds tae us like we should be exercisin first aid! He's hurt bad.

Bella Imagine it was you. Wouldn't you want help? I was brought up to help people!

Aria (*changing her mind*)   Maybe we should check? Just check. In case it's serious.

Tannoy STAY WHERE YOU ARE. AWAIT NEW INSTRUCTIONS.

David   We don't know who he is, like you said – he's probably infected.

Layla   My thoughts exactly. So, here's what we'll do.

Bella   You are not in charge!

She sits up.

David   You need to lie down! Lie down now, Bella!

Aria   We'll get punished! You need to lie down!

Bella *ignores them.*

Bella   Just cos you went to RADA, you think you're God's gift. (*Imitating* **Layla**.) We must all have the highest, impossible standards, mustn't we?

Layla   How *dare* you talk to me like that, you . . . you . . . pigeon-livered ratbag!

Bella (*as herself*)   A'd rather be a ratbag than a catastrophically shit actor!

David   Stay in character, Bella! We don't want to be punished again!

Tannoy   STAY WHERE YOU ARE. AWAIT NEW INSTRUCTIONS.

Peggy   ENOUGH! This is not the time to tear each other apart! Lie down, Bella!

Aria   We need to make a decision.

Bella *reluctantly lies down on her front with her hands behind her head.*

Bella   He could be bleeding to death or anything.

Layla   He could be bleeding? Exactly! His infected blood could be spilling out some nasty new variant all over the floor!

Hugo   A phone. He might have a phone!

Layla (*to* **Hugo**)   You go in there; we could all get taken out of the experiment.

Bella   We've been here for months – going slowly – terminally – mad. Getting kicked out this nightmare might be the best we can hope for.

There is a tense pause, while everyone thinks about what they should do.

Trevor (*screaming*)   Please! Somebody! The pain. PLEASE! I think I'm passing out!

Bella   We need to help him!

She stands up and runs through to the sleeping area.

David   No, Bella!

Layla (*as herself*)   She's a total liability! Hope she's next!

A shrieking alarm fills the room as the lights fade. The rest of the cast follow **Bella** *apart from* **Layla**. **Layla** *eventually runs after them.*

Scene Four

The Interrogation

Day one, thirty minutes later that afternoon. Everyone is now wearing clear disposable gloves and heavy-duty surgical masks. **Trevor** *has been tied to a chair with strips of ripped bed sheets. He also wears a surgical mask and disposable gloves. They all keep their distance from* **Trevor**. *He has been bleeding heavily from one nostril – his white mask is stained with blood.*

Tannoy   RETURN THE INTRUDER TO THE INCINERATOR ROOM IMMEDIATELY. OR YOU WILL BE PUNISHED.

Trevor *is dragged in from the bedroom by* **Aria**. *She has* **Trevor's** *camera around her neck and his rucksack on her back. The others follow them into the room.*

Trevor   You didn't need to draw blood!

Hugo *is holding a lateral flow test in his palm and watching it keenly for the result.*

Hugo   Stop whinging!

Aria   It's your own fault for struggling so much.

Trevor   I wasn't struggling!

Peggy   You were so. You're lucky Hugo didn't poke your eye out.

Aria (*to* **Bella**)   Told you. There's nothing wrong with him.

Bella   You said your leg was broken!

Trevor   Thought it was broken.

Layla   Surely you can tell if your leg is broken or not?

Aria   Exactly – there's nothing wrong with you! That makes you a liar.

Trevor   How does it? Was confused. Could have died falling through that!

Aria   Doubt it. You *luckily* fell directly onto a bed?

Trevor   Was . . . very lucky.

Aria   I wasn't. YOU BROKE MY BED!

She kicks **Trevor** *hard on the knee.*

David   Why did you say you were hurt?!

Trevor   I'm not meant to be here. Didn't plan to fall through the roof!

Hugo   No shit, Sherlock.

He finds his own joke funny but nobody else does. He goes back to watching the test develop but keeps an eye on the others.

Bella (*points to cameras*)   *They* are going be livid that we helped you.

Peggy   We broke so many rules for you, and for what?

Layla   You broke the rules, Bella! (*Shouts to a* **Tannoy**.)
We never!

Trevor (*to* **Peggy**)   You need to break the rules! All of them.
It's the only way you'll get out of here.

Bella (*bitterly*)   All for one and one for all, Layla – wasn't
that what we agreed that first night?

Layla   We live and learn. Especially when the champagne
runs out.

Bella *flips* **Layla** *the bird –* **Layla** *smiles back sarcastically.*

Peggy (*to* **Trevor**)   Trevor Rivers. Really? That's a crap name.

Maddie   Sounds like a makey-uppy name.

Peggy   Like a crap actor's name. Nobody – and I mean
NOBODY – is called Trevor!

Trevor   That's my name!

Peggy   You tricked us! That makes you a bad person.

Bella   Where are we?

Trevor   If I tell you – will you untie me? (*Indicating the straps
around his wrists.*) This isn't necessary!

David   Trevor, mate – don't try to bargain with them. You'll
just make it worse.

Trevor   Untie me first. Untie me. Tell you everything I know.

Aria *boots* **Trevor**'s *knee hard. He screams out in pain. She boots
his knee again.*

Aria   We want the truth!

Peggy (*to a* **Tannoy**)   And new blankets! And more food!
Can we exchange him for food?!

Trevor (*to* **Peggy**)   I'm a human being! Not some /

Bella   / Where are we?!

Trevor   An industrial complex. North of the capital. Beside the canal.

The group are taken aback by this news.

Aria (*to the others*)   The capital?

Bella   Thought we had to be out in the country. We were in and out of vans for hours and hours.

Aria   They must have drove us round in circles. To disorientate us. Bella. Could hardly breathe wearing that hood.

Peggy   And my hood stank of fish! I mean seriously – fish?!

David (*to* **Trevor**)   We haven't seen anyone new. Since the director left us.

Bella   Is it bad out there?

Peggy   Are people still dying?

Trevor   Yes. Well – no. What I mean is – yes. But no more than normal.

Maddie   If he lied aboot a broke leg, whit else'd he lie aboot? A dinnae trust him.

Tannoy   RETURN THE INTRUDER TO THE INCINERATOR ROOM IMMEDIATELY. OR YOU WILL BE PUNISHED.

Layla   There's still time to send him back! It's not our fault he fell through the skylight.

She tries to drag **Trevor** *towards the Incinerator Room.*

Layla   There's still time to get back on the straight and /

Bella   / Forget it!

She grabs **Layla** *by her hair and pulls her away from the chair.*

Bella   Not until we find out everything he knows.

David   That's enough, Bella!

Bella *throws* **Layla** *to the floor.*

Layla   You'll regret that.

Bella   Doubt it. I'm not scared of you, Layla. The only thing I'm really scared of is my own temper. Just remember that.

Peggy   If we don't give him back. Where's he going to sleep?

Aria   And we barely get enough to eat as it is.

Trevor   Can sleep in one of the spare beds. Just for tonight. Then I'll find a way to get back into the real world. Won't be any trouble. Don't send me out there!

Aria   How do you know we have spare beds?

Trevor   Or I can sleep on the floor. Listen. Look! You can't send me back out there. I'm not meant to be here. They'll hurt me.

Peggy *gets really uptight – like she's going to have a panic attack.*

Peggy   You can't stay! You're ruining it for everyone! (*To the group.*) He can't stay. We're in enough trouble as it is!

Aria   You'll sleep there – strapped into that chair. Until we figure out what we're going to do with you.

David   What's happening – out there?

Bella   The new lockdown. Is it over?

Trevor   There was no new lockdown. Just another brainwashing tactic. To keep you here. So you don't try to escape.

David   If he's not part of the experiment – how does he know about the spare beds?

Peggy   If he was part of the experiment and they sent him here – why would they want him back so badly?

Aria   What are you doing here?!

She boots **Trevor** *in the same knee again.*

Trevor   PLEASE! I TOLD YOU! I'm a freelance journalist. Trying to get some photographs of this. This experiment.

Aria   But why?!

Trevor   Been watching the show since the beginning. You are being exploited. Used.

Layla   Show?

Trevor   And I was worried. About the way they are treating you. So I started to do some research. You are just puppets in a /

David   / What show?!

Aria   This is a social experiment. An acting experiment.

Peggy   An academic experiment.

Trevor   You are being shown live on a new channel. A subscription channel. Twenty-four hours a day. It's called The Edge of Pain.

Bella   What is – the TV show?

Trevor   No – the channel.

David   What's the show called.

Trevor   The Dodo Experiment.

Layla   You must be mistaken. You mean The Pygmalion Experiment. This is The Pygmalion Experiment.

Trevor   To you it is.

He nods towards one of the cameras.

To them out there – this is The Dodo Experiment.

David   Why dodo?

Bella   Dead as a dodo?

A wave of fear ripples through them.

Peggy   Is theatre the dodo? Isn't that what this is all about? Seeing if we can breathe new life into dead art?

David   Dodos are extinct.

Hugo (*trying to be funny*)   I don't see any huge extinct pigeons flying about.

Maddie   Thay couldnae fly.

Hugo   *And?* (*Bullying.*) What?! You want a medal for knowing that?

Maddie *is hurt by this and walks away.*

Hugo   Didn't think so.

Peggy (*scared but getting angry*)   What's our names? If you know so much about us.

Trevor *points to each of them with his head as he says their names.*

Trevor   Hugo. Maddie. Aria. Layla. Peggy. David. Bella.

David   So it's like *Big Brother*?

Trevor   Sort of. The main difference is *Big Brother* ends. This doesn't.

Layla   Course it bloody ends!

Trevor   Check your contracts.

Peggy   We don't have our contracts.

David   We don't have anything.

Aria   They took everything from us.

The group looked blankly between each other.

David   Didn't read my contract. Not really. Was just delighted they wanted me.

Bella   Same here.

Aria   Same.

Peggy   Same.

Maddie   Me an aw.

Hugo   Didn't even open mine.

Layla *rolls her eyes at the unprofessionalism of everyone else. She pulls her contract out from under her dress. As she pulls out the contract a crushed and unopened packet of cigarettes, a Zippo lighter and some lighter fuel also fall out.*

Bella   Should have guessed.

Layla *quickly stuffs the cigarettes, lighter and lighter fuel back inside her dress.*

David   Didn't know you smoked.

Layla   I don't. These are . . . for emergencies.

Maddie   Whit else ye git hidin up thare?

Layla   A spade. To bury you with. After I've decapitated you with it!

Peggy   Layla! That sort of sniping is not helping the situation.

Layla (*smugly*)   I read my contract – regularly. From cover to cover. And I'm quite happy with it. Everything is above board.

Trevor   Read clause twenty-seven again.

Layla *flicks through the contract and reads out the clause.*

Layla   Here it is. Clause twenty-seven. 'Footage of this experiment will be used for research, education and . . . *entertainment* purposes'.

Aria (*to* **Layla**)   Did you know all along this was going to get broadcast?

Layla   Wasn't sure what 'entertainment' meant. But it didn't concern me. We're actors – some of us – I don't have any problem with being on camera. They document experiments all the time. That's how they evaluate. Anyway – we're only here for six months.

Trevor   At *least* six months.

Bella   What do you mean?

Trevor   Look it up. Clause eh-eh-eh thirty-six.

David   How do you know so much about our contracts?

Trevor   It was leaked. Onto the web. I've been through it with a fine-tooth comb. Clause six – no contact with friends or family. Clause seven – no intimacy. Clause forty-three – the management are not responsible for injury inflicted on subjects by other subjects. Clause one hundred and seven – payment of subject fees are at the *discretion* of the management on *satisfactory* completion of the experiment. Will I keep going?

Layla *flicks through her contract frantically.*

Aria (*to the group*)   We still don't know why he's here.

Layla *finds the section in her contract and scans it.*

Trevor (*to* **Aria**)   Started writing a blog. About what they are doing to you here. Was trying to take photos. To prove to the world young actors are being exploited right here in the capital. That's why I'm here. To document it. To prove that you're being treated inhumanly. Then I fell through.

David   Sounded to me like you were trying to break the glass on purpose.

Layla   He's right. It says '*at least* six months'. There's no end date.

Peggy (*to* **Hugo**)   What's the result of the lateral flow?

Hugo   The blood's making it hard to read. Not sure yet.

Bella   Look in his bag.

Trevor   Fine. I've nothing to hide.

Aria   Nice camera,

She takes the rucksack and rummages through it. She pulls out a mobile phone.

Aria   Cheap phone . . . looks broken.

She puts the camera and the phone down on the table beside **Hugo**'s *pile of wires and components. Then she continues to rummage through the rucksack. When* **Aria** *moves away* **Hugo** *goes over and inspects the phone and camera. He starts to dismantle the camera – he's looking for components to help him finish his project. He also keeps checking the lateral flow test for a final result.*

Aria   Empty bottle of water. *Pygmalion* script?! Why have you got this?

She holds the script up so the others can see it.

Trevor   To try to understand how this play fits in with what they are doing to you here.

David   Don't believe him.

Hugo   I say we send him back. Torture him first. Then send him back.

Bella   Anything else in the bag?

Aria   Nope.

Trevor   I've told you what I know. Can't feel my hands. Can you untie me, please?

Aria   Why should we?

Trevor   I can help you.

Aria   You keep saying that.

Tannoy   RETURN THE INTRUDER TO THE INCINERATOR ROOM IMMEDIATELY. OR YOU WILL BE PUNISHED.

Bella (*to* **Aria**)   He must be part of the experiment. Why else would he be here?

Trevor   Don't you see all this is wrong? You've all been isolated. From the rest of the world. They're trying to make you go crazy. They want you to destroy each other.

Peggy   Maybe he's right.

Layla   No! He's lying. I can feel it.

David   We must finish the experiment. We're contracted to finish it. And to be honest – I need the money.

Trevor   What money?! This ends when you end. This experiment is about the survival of the fittest. Nothing more – nothing less.

Layla   Don't listen to him. We stick it out!

Bella   We have been doing nothing but sticking it out for four bloody months.

She stands under a **Tannoy** *and shouts up.*

Bella   We want to speak to a lawyer! Now! We want to speak to a lawyer now! We are being held under false pretences. We are being exploited!

Hugo   So, what are we gonna do? With him?

Peggy   I say we give him the benefit of the doubt. He could be telling the truth.

David *studies* **Trevor***'s face up close like he's looking at a familiar painting.*

David   What's your name again?

Trevor   Told you. Trevor. Trevor Rivers.

David   Have we met before?

Trevor (*lying*)   Don't think so.

David   I'm sure I've met you somewhere. Recognise your face.

Trevor   Just got one of those faces. I'm everybody's doppelganger. (*Trying to have a joke with them.*) A human chameleon.

Aria   I hate reptiles. Are you cold blooded? Like a chameleon? We can check. I can go get one of those huge shards of glass sticking out of my bed and cut you with it. That'd be a good game wouldn't it?

Hugo   I'd play that game.

David   It will come to me. Definitely know you from somewhere. Are you an actor like us?

Trevor   I've told you! I'm a journalist. A freelance journalist.

Hugo   I've looked through his camera. There's no photos. Of anything. No memory card. It's empty.

Bella   Why would a real journalist be carrying an empty camera?

Trevor   The memory card. Must have fell out when I landed. It will be in there somewhere. The bed. The floor. Check!

David   We should vote.

Bella (*to* **Trevor**)   We vote on every big decision. It is the only way to keep a sense of order in here. After what happened.

Trevor   I know.

Aria   We need to meet – now!

Peggy *points to the sleeping area.*

Peggy   In there.

Aria   Away from prying ears.

They head for the sleeping area. Everyone follows, **David** *lags behind a bit as he is still trying to figure out where he has seen* **Trevor** *before, then joins the group.* **Hugo** *comes back in and grabs the lateral flow test before going into the sleeping area.*

Scene Five

Bad Blood

The early hours of day two. **Aria** *and* **Bella**'s *turn to watch* **Trevor**. **Bella** *peers up into the lens of one of the cameras.* **Aria** *is arguing with* **Trevor**. **Bella** *and* **Aria** *speak in their own accents.*

Aria   Just because you tested negative doesn't give you any privileges!

Trevor   Please! I need to go to the bathroom.

Aria   We don't have a bathroom! We don't even have a bucket. Now shut up. If you need to go that bad – go there.

She walks over to **Bella**. **Bella** *flips the camera the bird.*

Aria (*deadly serious*)   We need to make a final decision. As a group.

Bella   Hugo can't be allowed to abstain again.

Aria (*about* **Hugo**)   Don't trust gadget boy. He's hedging his bets. Don't trust anyone.

Bella   I'd trust you before I'd trust them. And that's saying something.

Aria (*tired and drained*)   Just want all this to stop.

Trevor   I can get it to stop.

Aria   And how are you going to do that? Dig us a tunnel with cake forks?

There's an awkward silence.

Trevor (*changing the subject*)   Does this place remind you of your student days. You know, crap hygiene, crap mental health, crap maintenance, crap meals, crap present, crap future, crap fridges, crap roommates.

Bella   Excuse me?

Trevor   You need to trust your roommates. If you can't trust them – who can you trust?

Aria   What did you mean by that?

She kicks the knee she was kicking before. **Trevor** *screams out in pain.*

Aria   Stop whining – people are trying to sleep in there.

Trevor (*whispering*)   You keep doing that and you'll break my kneecap.

Aria (*whispering back sarcastically*)   Trust me. A broken kneecap is nothing compared to a broken heart! You men are all the same. Weak.

She lifts her foot as if she's going to kick **Trevor** *again.*

Bella   What else do you know about us?

Trevor   Researched all of you. Hugo's made a fortune designing free torture games. Peggy is under a restraining order for stalking. Maddie recently served a six-month suspended sentence for fraud. Oh – Bella. You'll like this. And Layla went to the Reading Arts and Drama Association's summer school two years ago – other than that she's only done am dram and worked full time in a Tesco call centre.

Bella   Bloody knew it.

Aria   What about us?

Trevor   Roommates in college. Besties, by the sounds of it. Haven't spoken in years.

Bella   That's none of your business.

Aria   Why are you so interested?

Bella   Answer her question.

Trevor (*uses his head to point to a* **Tannoy**)   You're being exploited and abused by them for money. I want to help.

Aria   So you say.

Bella (*suspicious*)   Still don't know how you found us. It's too quiet around here for us to be in the city. So why can't we hear any cars. Listen.

Bella *and* **Aria** *listen.*

Trevor   This place has thick walls.

Bella (*losing her patience*)   There's a massive hole in the bloody roof!

Trevor *needs to distract them from this train of thought so reveals one of his ace cards.*

Trevor   Listen! It's much worse than you think. Didn't want to. You two need to know this. Found out where you are through the IP address. From a Dark Web website. That's where the show is broadcast from.

Bella   What website?

Aria   You said it was a bloody subscription service.

Bella   Like Amazon Prime or something.

Trevor   It is. Sort of. Didn't want to freak everyone out before. It's on the Dark Web.

Bella   Dark bloody web. Don't be ridiculous,

Aria   Does that even exist?

Bella   Are you taking the /

Trevor   / People pay to watch you get humiliated – hurt. That's why I can't go out there. They're bad people. Sick in the head. The last thing they need is me poking my nose in. Exposing them.

Aria   If it is on the Dark Web. How did you find out about it?

Trevor *avoids answering* **Aria**.

Trevor   This is making them a fortune. Sickos, fascists, incels, sadists – all the world's maggots are addicted to the show, especially when they see what happens to actors that act up.

Bella   Answer her question.

Trevor   Chat forums. There's even memes of the missing actors out there.

Aria *tries to look into the Incinerator Room.*

Aria   Maddie thinks they got incinerated.

Bella   Maddie thinks a lot of things.

Aria *looks at a* **Tannoy** *then a camera warily.*

Aria   I don't want to be on the Dark Web.

Bella   Maybe we haven't seen the half of it yet.

Aria   If you are telling us the truth – you should know what happened to them. That night.

Trevor   The last thing we saw was them going into there.

He indicates the Incinerator Room with his head and body.

As far as I know they never came out. Only Platinum subscribers get to watch what happens in the Incinerator Room.

Aria (*innocently*)   Why would anybody pay to watch rubbish burn?

Trevor   This isn't an experiment. It's a blood sport.

Bella   You better not be lying to us!

Aria   I have nowhere to sleep because you DESTROYED MY BED!

She has been moaning endlessly about her broken bed up to this point – **Bella** *can't take it anymore.*

Bella   Oh my God, you're lucky you weren't in it when he landed. Why can't you just clean your bed and stop griping!

Aria   Why should I? It wasn't me who broke it!

Bella   Take a spare bed.

Aria   I don't want to sleep in a spare bed!

Bella   Wow – you haven't changed one bit!

Aria   What do you mean?

Bella   Even back in college, nothing was ever your fault.

Aria   Not this again. I wasn't paying forty quid for something that wasn't my fault. Simple.

Bella   Simple? Really? So it was okay that I had to fork out eight hundred because the fridge *accidentally* did a back flip out of the kitchen window – just because you didn't want to pay your half – your forty quid – to get it fixed?! You killed Tina!

Aria   I told you not to overload it, buying all that reduced fruit as if apple trees were gonna die out – then leaving it all to rot! It was disgusting.

Trevor (*laughing*)   Wait, you didn't speak for years over a *fridge*?

Aria   Yes. After it fell out the window. Onto her car.

Bella   Tina was more than a car to me – she was a friend! Aria thought the fridge would be covered by the landlord's insurance. It wasn't.

Aria   So she set fire to my bed.

Bella   Allegedly!

Aria   When I was in it.

Bella   You are still the same. Always need to exaggerate. (*To* **Trevor**.) She wasn't in the bed.

Aria   Whatever.

She inspects the cameras again.

Bella (*winding up* **Aria**)   Bet your ex watches this.

Aria   Wouldn't put it past him. (*Directly to a camera.*) If by any chance you're watching this. I hate you! You two-timing cretin! When I told you that birthmark on your back was sexy? I LIED! It looks like a cheesy beano! Scumbag.

She gestures rudely and repeatedly to the camera before getting bored and sitting on a chair. There's an uncomfortable silence.

Trevor   The riot night? They didn't broadcast all of that.

Aria   We went crazy.

Bella   There were fights.

Aria (*whispers*)   Sexual dalliances.

Bella   Bullying.

Aria (*points to* **Tannoy**)   They started it! They cut the heating, and we weren't happy with dinner. It was chippy pickles. Every meal is someone's favourite food.

Bella   Sounds great on paper right?

Aria   But when we saw it was chippy pickled onions again for the third day in a row, well . . .

Bella   We'd had enough. The gin was there so we thought, eff it, let's get melted.

Aria   It is all a bit blurry after that.

Bella   Druggy blurry.

Aria   We think the gin was spiked. It must have been.

Bella   In the morning when we woke up the others were gone.

Aria (*sarcastically*)   And everybody lived happily ever after.

She boots **Trevor** *hard on his knee. He winces in pain.*

Aria   Right then, Trevor. Tell us. What is this grand plan of yours?

Trevor (*seriously*)   We burn the building down.

Scene Six

Singing for Their Supper

Day two, dinner time. **Hugo** *is engrossed in his pile of wires and components.* **Trevor** *is sleeping and still tied to the chair. Everyone else stands up or enters the space. They are all very mannerly with each other as they stand behind their chairs at the perfectly laid dinner table. The cast stand and formally sing 'Land of Hope and Glory' until a soft light comes on indicating that they should take their seats and their food is ready to serve.* **Bella** *and* **Aria** *watch the others carefully and exchange looks throughout this scene – they have agreed a plan with* **Trevor** *but are worried the others might find out.*

All

Land of hope and glory
Mother of the free
How shall we extol thee
Who are born of thee
Wider still and wider
Shall thy bounds be set
God who made thee mighty
Make thee mightier
God who made thee mighty
Make thee mightier yet

The cast sit as for a formal dinner. **Maddie**, *wearing disposable gloves and an industrial face mask, lights the candles in the candelabras before bringing in a silver platter covered with a domed lid. She picks up a silver jug on the table and pours everyone a glass of water. She then lifts the domed lid and they are shocked to see they have only one packet of ready salted crisps between them.*

Maddie   Dinner is served. Apparently.

She solemnly snips the crisp bag open with a pair of silver scissors before pouring the crisps onto the silver tray as she hums 'Land of Hope and Glory'. She takes a pair of silver tongs and places a crisp on each person's plate. She repeats this until all the crisps are distributed. She leaves them as they attempt to eat the crisps using cutlery. She goes over and sits close to **Trevor**.

David   Nothing for breakfast again – and now this!

Hugo   This is a joke, right? We normally get a packet each!

Bella   The whole thing's a big bloody joke. Has been from the bloody start.

Layla   No it has not! We are just being punished because you broke the rules!

Bella   They've been punishing us since we arrived.

Peggy   Before we arrived! Blindfolded. Manhandled. Wanted to scream when we were in the back of those vans. Was too scared – so I just screamed over and over in my head.

Aria   Me too.

Bella   We've just been too desperate to complain.

Aria   Up until now that is.

Bella   Trevor the skydiving journalist has done us all a favour.

Aria   We need to take control of this situation.

Layla   We must know our place!

Aria   Why must we?

David (*pointing to a* **Tannoy**)   No point getting them angry again. Remember what happened the last time.

Peggy   We shouldn't talk about those things!

Layla   She's right. Certain subjects should not be discussed at the dinner table. Now please. Be quiet. Nature will castigate those who don't masticate.

Bella (*mocking* **Layla**)   Nature will castigate those who don't masticate.

They sit in silence mindfully chewing on each sliver of crisp thirty-two times as they try in vain to be mannerly.

Trevor (*to* **Maddie**)   That's one of the bits I hate the most about all this. The way you need to sit in the corner and eat their scraps. It's just not right.

Maddie   A'm juist the Scottish maid – maids dinnae git tae eat at the dinner table.

Trevor   When do you think you'll get out of here?

Maddie   When we finish the play A suppose.

Trevor   How can you finish the play without the other actors?

Maddie (*animated*)   That's whit A keep sayin tae thaim – bit naebody listens.

Trevor   I'm listening. If you help me; I can help you. Help you stand up for yourself a bit better. You want to get out of here – right?

Maddie   Might dae.

She studies **Trevor**'*s face – deciding whether to trust him or not.*

Hugo   Can someone please pass the salt?

David   They're ready salted.

Hugo   And?

He stands up and leans over and grabs the salt cellar. He pours loads of salt onto his crisps. The others watch in disbelief.

Peggy   That can't be good for you.

Hugo (*not seeing what the problem is*)   What?!

David (*to* **Hugo** – *changing the subject*)   How you getting on with that . . . that . . . thingamabob you are tinkering with?

David *points to pile of wires and dismantled components on the chair at the back of the room.*

Hugo   Nearly there. Just need to figure out how to boost the power.

Layla (*trying to be engaged and charming*)   Oh your science experiment! Please. Do tell us more, Hugo. You, you, you little inventor you. Will it make us rich?

Hugo *ignores* **Layla** *and pretends to be focused on trying to cut up a crisp. The main group falls into an awkward silence.*

Maddie   If yer tryin tae sook in wi us – forget it. Ye're tied tae a chair. At any point any wan ae thaim coud pit that plastic bag ower yer heid.

She points to a plastic bag on the floor.

An that'd be that. Nae offence bit you offerin tae listen tae us disnae mak us feel ony less ae the maid.

She bites her nails and thinks about the consequences of her next question.

Maddie   Daed ye see whit really happent? On the telly? That night?

Trevor   The night the other actors went missing?

Maddie   Aye. A drank that much gin A blacked oot. (*Whispering.*) We think (*pointing to a* **Tannoy**) *they* drugged us.

Trevor   They wanted you all to argue more. That's why they started delivering six bottles of gin every morning like it was milk. They knew all that booze and tiredness would bring out the worst in everyone. You fell asleep in the corner over there. The other three actors stayed up. Drinking more and more. Then they tried break into the Incinerator Room – they wanted to go home. They attacked the door of the Incinerator Room with everything they could. Chairs, bottles, shoes. The rest of you were so smashed that you all slept through it. Then. The door to the Incinerator Room opened. They stepped in and closed the door behind them.

Aria *slams her cutlery down on her plate.*

Aria (*breaking*)   We can't go on like this!

Peggy   I wholeheartedly agree. It's not . . . healthy.

They sit staring at their plates looking distraught. **David** *eventually breaks the silence.*

David   Kebab meat with cheese. And curry sauce. *And* gravy. That would go some way to feeding the ravenous gargoyle in my gut.

Everyone at the table fantasises about their favourite foods as they try to eat a crisp politely with a knife and fork.

Layla   Toad in the hole.

Bella   Grilled chicken Caesar salad.

Hugo   A Curly Wurly.

Peggy   A packet of raw bacon – straight from the fridge!

Everybody looks at her in shock. They all take a drink of water.

Layla   Are you pregnant?

Peggy   Don't be ridiculous. I just like chilled, sliced flesh.

They continue to sit in silence, masticating – not knowing what to say.

Maddie   So they escaped?

Trevor   I never said that. They stepped into that room. They stepped into that room and never came out.

He starts laughing. **Maddie** *gets annoyed.*

Maddie   A dinnae ken how yer laughin. If A wis you – tied tae a chair in this madhoose – ye widnae sec us laughin.

Trevor   Look at them all. Sitting there – oblivious.

Maddie   Oblivious tae whit?

Trevor   Doesn't matter.

Maddie   Oblivious tae whit?!

Trevor   If I tell you – you'll just tell them.

Maddie   How wad A tell any ae thaim? Dinnae even like thaim.

Trevor   But if you did. Well. I don't know what might happen next. Things could get sticky.

Maddie   Listen, Trev – ye're a hostage. Things're awready a wee bit sticky toffee puddin. Tell us. A promise on ma life. A'll keep it a secret. (*Whispers.*) A'm needin tae ken!

Trevor   It's nothing. Forget A said it.

Maddie (*getting frustrated*)   Whit if A pit that plastic bag ower yer heid an set fire tae it? Wid that jog yer memory?

Trevor *thinks he can call her bluff.*

Trevor   Do it.

Maddie   Think A willnae?

Maddie *shows the plastic bag to* **Trevor**.

Maddie   A mean it!

Trevor   You don't have the bottle. You can't even stand up for yourself with those idiots over there.

Maddie   Fine!

She places the plastic bag over **Trevor**'s *head. She then takes the matches she used to light the candles from her pocket and shakes them at the side of* **Trevor**'s *head.*

Maddie   Juist acause A'm Scottish – iverybody 'hinks A'm mental. But that's because A actually um mental. Nou tell us whit's sae funny or A swear A'll /

Trevor   / The water! They don't drug the gin. The water. They drug the water!

Maddie *pulls the bag off* **Trevor**'s *head.*

Maddie   Say that again.

Trevor   They drug the water.

Maddie   Who dis?

Trevor   They do!

Maddie   Whit dae the drugs dae?

Trevor   They make you compliant. They make you do whatever they say. Look. Why else would they be allowing themselves to be humiliated like this?

Maddie   Ye cannae prove that.

Trevor   I don't need to prove anything. Use your own eyes! None of them will get out of here. Me and you. Me and you we can make /

Maddie (*shouts*)   / STOP!

She hurries over to the table.

Maddie   Thay dinnae drug the gin. Thay drug the watter! Dinnae drink it! The watter's drugged!

Peggy's *face lights up at the thought of being able to drink the gin.*

Peggy   Dirty martini, anyone?

Scene Seven

Boiled Trev and Carrots

The early hours of day three. Swigging gin from a bottle, a sloshed **Peggy** *is shouting back at the group in the sleeping area who are grumbling and trying to sleep.*

Peggy   Middle of the night my bare arse! We are theatricals! We are meant to be lushes – reprobates – party animals. Wake up, David! Don't be a lightweight. The night is young! And we are young! And I intend to devour the night like it is a, a, a . . . fried liver toastie!

She sings 'Boiled Beef and Carrots' as she does a cheeky vaudevillian dance around the room. **Trevor** *watches* **Peggy** *warily.*

Peggy (*spiteful*)
   When I was a nipper only six months old
   My mother and my father, too
   They didn't know what to wean me on
   They were in a dreadful stew
   They thought of tripe, they thought of steak
   Or a little bit of old cod row
   I said, 'Pop round to the old cook-shop
   And I tell ya what'll make me grow'
   Boiled beef and carrots
   Boiled beef and carrots
   That's the stuff for your 'darby-kell'
   Makes you fat and it keeps you well
   Don't live like vegetarians
   Or food they give to parrots
   Blow out your kite from morn' till night
   On boiled beef and carrots

She goes over to **Trevor** *and points at the bottle.*

Peggy   See this? This here? This is the good stuff.

She takes a glug and screws up her face. She reads the label.

Forty-three point one per cent alcohol. That's very precise isn't it? How do you measure point one per cent? They could be lying. How would we ever know. They could be barefaced liars. Just. Like. You!

She takes a long glug of gin.

Trevor   Maybe you should slow down. You don't need any more gin, you're practically a bottle in human form as it is.

Peggy (*as* **Eliza**)   They all thought she was dead; but my father he kept ladling gin down her throat til she came to so sudden that she bit the bowl off the spoon. What call would a woman with that strength in her have to die of influenza? What become of her new straw hat that should have come to me? Somebody pinched it; and what I say is, them as pinched it done her in.

She bows theatrically before going over to a **Tannoy**.

Peggy (*shouting at a* **Tannoy** *speaker*)   Little Tannoy experiment woman! We don't want him here! He's an imposter! I've known that from the start. He says you are drugging us! Why would you drug us? We're the stars of the show! We'll swap him. For a director – and a hog roast. With chips! And mayonnaise. *Hellmann's* mayonnaise – not that cheap rubbish in they wee impenetrable sachets that looks and tastes like emulsion paint! On no-no-no-no-no. It has to be Hellmann's! Will you have a drink with me, Trev, old chap? My drinking buddy seems to have passed out.

Trevor   They'll let you all go mad. Slowly starve to death. You do know that don't you?

Peggy   I won't starve. I'd eat you first. I'm sure we all would. The outcast always goes in the pot first – it's tradition. If it comes to dying of starvation or eating you? You. Are. Getting it.

(*Sings.*)
    Boiled Trev and carrots.
    Boiled Trev and carrots
    Don't live like vegetarians
    Or food they give to parrots
    Blow out your kite from morn' till night
    On boiled Trev and carrots

She laughs at her own joke.

Oh my God. Sometimes I'm actually effen hilarious.

Trevor   I'd clap – but my hands are tied. If you could just /

Peggy   / Nice try, Trev. This would make a good improvisation exercise. This. Don't you think? You know – you tied. Me – tipsy. Will you be able to persuade me – get me to untie you? Improvisations are all fine and good but they are so much sharper – so much more effective – when overseen by a good director. The answer's no!

Trevor   She's never coming back.

Peggy   Who?

Trevor   To direct the play.

Peggy   Of course she is! Why else would we still be here?!

Trevor   That's because she doesn't direct plays.

Peggy   Of course she does!

Trevor   She's part of the trap. She couldn't direct a play for the stage if she wanted to. It's a different skillset entirely.

Peggy   What is? You don't know what you're talking /

Trevor   / She's a film director! A documentary film director. Down on her luck like all of you are. She's watching everything through these cameras. She's been directing the whole thing – through these cameras. From up there. From the beginning. She tricked you. Betrayed you. Don't you recognise her voice?

She makes the Tannoy announcements. You send me back to her and you're playing straight into their /

Peggy   / You are such a liar!

Trevor   WHY WOULD I LIE?

He has a coughing fit.

Scene Eight

Rebellion

The afternoon of day three. Everyone is now speaking in their own accents apart from **Layla**. **Hugo** *is sitting beside his pile of wires and components with the rest of the group surrounding him. He looks a bit shaken up. The group has now clearly split down the middle with* **Layla**, **David** *and* **Peggy** *in one camp and* **Maddie**, **Bella** *and* **Aria** *in the other.* **Peggy** *is sick with a hangover that borders on alcohol poisoning. She spends most of the scene with her* *head in an empty black bin bag dry retching.* **Trevor** *coughs throughout the scene.* **David** *is sipping gin from a bottle.*

David   Just feed him to the lions. He's caused nothing but trouble!

Hugo   This isn't exactly an easy decision!

Aria   Stop procrastinating!

Maddie (*impatiently*)   Whit if A stick yer heid in this bag?

She holds up the plastic bag and matches that she used to threaten **Trevor** *with earlier.*

Maddie   Wid that help ye tae focus?!

She shakes the matches at **Hugo**.

Peggy   Maddie, there's no need to be so nasty.

Bella *snatches the matches out of* **Maddie**'s *hand and throws them to* **Aria**.

Maddie   Thay're mine!

Bella   I'll sleep better tonight knowing they're now hers.

Maddie   Cheek ae ye. Ye'll be lightin yer ain caunles fae nou on!

Aria (*aside to* **Bella**)   We'll be lighting more than candles.

Layla   What do you mean by that?

Bella (*to* **Layla**)   You snore and fart all night long – did you know that? When you are sleeping, we light your farts.

Layla   Idiots.

Peggy   Maybe Hugo just needs more time. To outweigh – I mean weigh up – the pros and cons. Make a list.

Layla (*to* **Hugo**)   Add this to your list – where's the memory card for his camera – eh? Did we ever find it?

Bella   Not finding it – doesn't mean it isn't still lost somewhere!

Aria   We didn't look properly. Could be in amongst the glass on my old bed.

David (*intimidating* **Trevor**)   Still weird it wasn't in the camera though – eh?

Aria   This isn't getting us anywhere.

She stomps off into the sleeping area.

Trevor   Can I state my case?

Layla   NO!

David   Not again!

Layla   Sick of the sound of your voice.

Peggy (*to* **Trevor**)   This is between us – stay out of it!

Aria *enters with a massive shard of glass. The bottom of the shard has material wrapped around it to create a handle. She points the makeshift knife at* **Hugo**'s *neck.*

Aria   You are going to decide RIGHT NOW.

David   What do you think you are playing at, Aria!

Aria   DECIDE!

She holds the glass even closer to **Hugo**'s *neck.*

Hugo (*defiantly*)   Or what?

Aria   YES OR NO!?

Peggy   Stop it! This is going too far! This is /

She vomits into the bin bag.

Hugo   / Listen to Peggy – stop being a psycho.

Aria   You want to see a psycho?!

Maddie   Calm yersel doun – that's enough, Aria.

Aria   Is it? (*To* **Hugo.**) VOTE! Or I swear I'll /

Tannoy. / ATTENTION. YOU MUST CHOOSE ONE
ACTOR TO ENTER THE INCINERATOR ROOM
IMMEDIATELY. IF YOU REFUSE TO DO THIS YOU
WILL BE SEVERELY PUNISHED.

Bella   See? See! That's them trying to mess with our heads
again.

Aria   Ignore them.

*They look at each other – they are scared, and no one wants to make
the first move. Eventually* **Layla** *breaks the silence.*

Layla   Well, I know who I'm choosing.

She points to **Bella**.

Peggy (*shocked*)   You're actually going to choose to send one
of us to the Incinerator Room? (*Pointing to* **Trevor**.) He's
different – he's not one of us. I understand throwing him
under a bus. But not one of us?!

Layla   We need to do as they say. We need to eat!

Bella   We don't even know what happens in there!

Maddie   Fire, fire, an mair fire, bi the sounds ae it.

David   Bella – it needs to be you. You're just too . . .
unpredictable.

Bella   You don't mean that. It could kill someone going in
there.

David   As far as I can see? We're dead anyway.

*He takes a long slug from a bottle of gin before sitting down at the
dinner table. He keeps sipping from the bottle during the rest of the
scene.*

Aria   Nobody goes anywhere.

Bella (*pointing to* **Tannoy**)   We can't trust them!

Hugo   What do we do then?!

Trevor   We need to burn our way out.

Layla   Burn our way out? (*To* **David**.) Are you listening to this idiocy?

Aria   It's the only way to escape.

Trevor   A fire big enough and hot enough to set off all the alarms.

Aria   In the entire complex.

Bella   Hot enough to set off all the sprinklers.

Trevor   And automatically open the emergency doors.

Aria   Then we run.

Maddie   Sounds too easy.

Peggy   Or too dangerous. What if the emergency exits don't open?!

Bella   At least the sprinklers come on.

David   How's that going to help us?!

Bella   We'll get fresh water. We won't survive another day without water! We can fill up cups, jugs.

Trevor   She's right.

Peggy   What good is water without food!

Bella (*weakly*)   Buy some time for a Plan B? There's no way they can drug the water coming out the sprinklers – (*doubting herself*) can they?

Layla   This is ridiculous. Let's just give them Bella or Trevor. Or both. It's the obvious choice.

Bella   Obvious choice?!

Layla   This is all your fault. And trust me – no one will miss you.

Peggy   Don't be cruel, Layla.

Bella   They are expecting us to sacrifice one of the group? Just like that? And you want to keep pandering to them?! (*Sarcastically.*) *Every little helps*, I suppose – eh, Layla?

Layla *snaps at this dig at her working for Tesco – she snatches the carving knife off the table. She grabs* **Bella** *with her collar and holds her knife to* **Bella**'s *throat.*

Layla   You're nothing but a troublemaker!

She forces **Bella** *towards the Incinerator Room.*

Peggy   Layla, stop it! That's enough! Please, stop it!

Layla (*to* **Tannoy**)   Okay, we've chosen someone!

Aria   NO WE HAVEN'T.

She stands in front of **Layla** *– she holds out the shard of glass to stop her edging* **Bella** *over to the Incinerator Room.*

Aria   Don't want to hurt you Hugo but I will. We need a decision.

Hugo   I don't . . . know.

Peggy   The quicker you decide, the quicker this is all over.

Maddie   People are gonnae git hurtit. Either wey!

Aria   JUST MAKE A DECISION!

David   Aye, mate, it's not hard. Him . . . or her. Or both.

Aria   Let Bella go, Layla.

Layla   Not until decisions are made.

She shoots a look at **Hugo**.

David   Eeny, meeny, miny, moe.

Peggy   Please, Hugo. Make the choice. Vote!

All   Come on / Vote / Make a decision / We've waited long enough /

We've no time for this. (*Etc.*)

Hugo   OKAY! OKAY! Just send him back!

Trevor   WHAT? No. Don't. I can help you!

Layla (*to* **Tannoy**)   You heard Hugo, we are sending the intruder back! We are so very sorry for the delay and inconvenience our . . . *indecision* may have caused.

David *claps in approval.*

David (*to* **Hugo**)   Good choice, Hugo. At least one person's coming to their senses. Marvellous. About bloody time. I'll drink to that.

He swigs from the bottle.

Maddie (*to* **Layla**)   Awright, he made the choice. Leave her alane.

Layla   No. They want her too.

Bella   They never said that!

Aria   THAT'S IT! You touch her and I'll stick this in your neck!

She holds her piece of glass towards **Layla**.

Peggy (*really upset*)   Murdering each other won't get you anywhere! Stop this!

Trevor   Look what they are turning you into!

Layla   He goes back now! He's a snake in the grass. I just know it!

She points the carving knife at **Trevor**. **Maddie** *goes up behind* **Layla** *and* snatches *the carving knife out of her hand.* **Maddie** *cuts her hand badly when she grabs the blade.*

Bella (*threatening* **Layla**)   Don't you *ever* try anything like that again.

Layla *pushes past* **Bella**.

Maddie   A'm cut!

She grabs a linen napkin from the dining table and makes a makeshift bandage – no one helps her.

David   Right – Trev. You are going in the big, bad fire.

He starts to drag **Trevor** *towards the Incinerator Room.*

Peggy   Wait! No he's not. I'm changing my vote! Trevor stays. Bella stays.

David   You're making a huge mistake.

Peggy   I don't want anyone else getting hurt. This is a shambles. A disaster! The director's gone. She's never coming back. It's over.

Aria   She's right. We are being exploited!

Layla   That's just your hangover talking, Peggy!

Peggy   Most definitely.

She throws up into the bin bag.

Aria   Seconded.

Bella   Me too. He stays.

Layla *drops her* Pygmalion *accent from now on. She realises she's no longer in a position of power in the group.*

Layla   You're threatening our safety! Who knows what they'll do to punish us now!

She is scared and takes a strip of a bed sheet from the floor and grabs a bottle of gin. She throws away the cork and stuffs the strip of sheet into the top of the bottle. She takes the can of lighter fuel and squirts it onto the strip of sheet.

David   What are you doing, Layla?

She flips open the Zippo lighter, so it is ready to ignite.

Layla   What does it look like! For self-defence. Can't you see they're ganging up on us?

David *realises things are getting serious and picks up the fish knife from his place setting. He keeps it in his hand until the end of the play.*

Layla   We need to be ready.

Aria (*to* **Tannoy**)   We have made our decision.

Bella   Trev the intruder stays.

Maddie *cuts the strips of cloth connecting* **Trevor** *to the chair.*

Maddie   Majority rules.

When **Trevor** *stands up, he's wobbly and needs to lean on the chair.*

Trevor   Promise you. Together we can get out of here. Tomorrow we act.

Layla (*trying to save face*)   He doesn't get to sleep in there with us.

Trevor   Suits me fine.

Aria   Tomorrow. We act.

Bella (*shouts at* **Tannoy**)   No more bloody *Pygmalion*! The Dodo Experiment is over! We are /

She is cut off by a deafening and upsetting alarm and flashing lights that make everyone scream in agony. The stage darkens.

Scene Nine

Better the Devil You Know

Just before midnight on day three. Everyone is sleeping in the sleeping area apart from **Trevor** *who is curled up in the corner of the room wrapped in a blanket.* **Hugo** *comes in and sits down at his pile of wires and components. He fiddles with some wire connections – eventually we hear a weak, intermittent and distorted recording of a government announcement coming through.* **Hugo** *looks round to see if* **Trevor** *is awake – he is but pretends to be asleep.*

Government Announcer   No fuel. Bodies in the streets. New variant. Digging pits. Martial law. Stay inside. Power cuts. Families torn apart.

The signal fades and **Hugo** *tries desperately to get it back. He can't get it working so he heads back into the sleeping area. We hear muffled whispering from the sleeping area as* **Hugo** *tries to wake the rest of the group without waking* **Trevor**. *Once* **Trevor** *hears* **Hugo** *whispering with the others, he gets up silently.* **Trevor** *knows his lies are unravelling – he goes to the door of the Incinerator Room and quietly punches in the numbers two, six, zero, seven, one, eight, five, six. We hear a buzz, indicating it is the wrong code.*

He pulls at the door, but it doesn't open. He punches the numbers in again and it doesn't open. He pulls harder.

Trevor (*whispering to a* **Tannoy**)   Don't do this. It's time.

He punches in the numbers again.

Trevor   Two, six, zero, seven, one, eight, five, six. That's the right code. Pressing the right numbers. I did it! I DID WHAT YOU ASKED!

He furiously punches the code into the keypad of the door to the Incinerator Room. He tries frantically to pull the door open after each attempt. We hear a buzz each time, indicating it's wrong. The rest of the group stumble in. **David** *is slugging from a gin bottle.* **Layla** *carries a lighter in one hand and the bottle of gin with the rag hanging from it in the other hand.* **Maddie** *has the carving knife and* **Aria** *has the large shard of glass.*

David   What are you doing?

Trevor (*whispering*)   I saw someone moving in there. We need to act now. They are planning something.

Layla   Not the only ones – eh, Trevor?

Aria   Who were you shouting at?

Hugo   Pretending to be asleep that whole time?

Peggy   You were trying to escape.

Aria *points the shard of glass at* **Trevor**.

Aria   That's not part of the plan!

Trevor   No – no. They're up to something. In there!

Hugo   Full lockdown out there eh, Trev?

David   More shootings.

Aria   Martial law?!

Layla   You lied to us.

David   It's gotten worse out there. Hasn't it?!

Trevor (*pleading*)   There are fake broadcasts all the time now. Foreign agencies telling lies. Don't get taken in by them!

David *points his knife towards* **Trevor**.

David   STOP LYING!

Bella (*to* **Hugo**)   Why should we believe you?

Peggy (*to* **Hugo**, *pointing to the makeshift radio*)   Show us. We should all hear it for ourselves.

Hugo   I'll try.

He goes back and tinkers with the radio again – trying to get a signal.

Bella (*weakly defending* **Trevor**)   Everyone lies in here. Why would Hugo be any different?

Hugo   I'm not lying.

Aria (*to* **Trevor**)   Somebody has to be.

They all share a moment of stalemate in silence.

Bella   Hear that?

Peggy   Can't hear anything.

Bella   Exactly. That's why it's so quiet out there. (*To* **Trevor**.) You didn't lie about that. We are in the city – aren't we?

David   Have you had a code to get out of here this whole time?!

Trevor   NO! Well, yeah. Well, not really.

David   I'M FED UP OF YOUR LIES. WHICH IS IT?!

He throws a chair at **Trevor** *narrowly missing him.*

Trevor   YES, OKAY! Well, at least I thought I did. They gave me the wrong code!

Bella *and* **Aria** *exchange panicked glances.* **Bella** *goes over to the table and picks up her steak knife.*

Bella   Can't take much more of this.

David   Who did?!

Maddie   The experiment?

Aria   Why would they give you a code? You're a journalist.

Bella (*livid*)   Are you here just to betray us?!

Bella points *the steak knife at* **Trevor**.

Peggy   ANSWER HER!

Trevor   You all stopped drinking. The show got boring. They sent me in here to mess with your heads. Get the show trending on illegal notice boards again. Get you to implode.

David   But why us? Why pick us in the first place?!

Trevor   Your auditions were also a psychological assessment. All of you were diagnosed as being mentally unstable.

Bella   Of course we're unstable. We're bloody actors!!

She slashes out at **Trevor** *with the steak knife and cuts his cheek open.*

Trevor *screams and holds his hand to his cheek. Blood oozes through his fingers.* **Bella** *can't believe what she's done and throws the knife to the floor. She grabs a bottle of gin and takes a massive swig.*

Bella (*frightened*)   We should kill you. If this was a movie – if this was a movie we'd descend upon you like a pack of wolves.

David   She's right.

Trevor   Can't you see that's what they want to happen?!

Maddie (*about* **Trevor**)   He's right.

Aria   Crashing through the skylight was a bit over the top – don't you think, Trev?!

Trevor   They wanted a dramatic entrance.

Layla   We definitely got that.

Maddie   Whit wis the code?

Trevor   His birthday.

David   Whose birthday?

Trevor   George Bernard Shaw's. Two, six, zero, seven, one, eight, five, six.

Maddie *goes over to the door and tries the code again. We hear a buzz, indicating it's wrong.*

Trevor (*pleading with the group*)   I'm just as trapped as you now. A victim like you now. A struggling actor like you.

David   That's it! I remember. Where I saw you. Knew I'd seen you.

After my audition. Was sitting on the steps outside. Hyperventilating into my rucksack. You stopped. You laughed and said, 'You might need this'. You dropped a used paper hankie right into my rucksack. Watched you as you glided smugly, confidently, through the revolving door. Didn't trust you then. Don't trust you now.

Trevor   I auditioned for Freddy. They gave me Trevor!

Peggy (*bitterly*)   And what a performance.

Aria   Bravo, ratbag!

Bella *holds her head in fear and frustration.*

Bella   Don't know what to believe any more.

Trevor   Why would I lie to you all now?!

Bella (*sarcastically*)   Force of habit, maybe?

Trevor   My real name is Marcus. Marcus Oates.

Layla   I believe him.

David   Me too.

Layla   But I don't trust him

Bella *grabs a crate of gin.*

Bella   Stuff this. I'm sticking with the plan.

Aria *throws the box of matches to* **Bella** *– she catches them.*

Aria   Me too.

Layla   We didn't agree to any burning! We still need to vote on that!

Aria *grabs a bottle of gin and walking backwards follows* **Bella** *into the sleeping area.*

Aria   I declare this democratic ensemble dissolved.

Trevor   Aria! Bella! Stop, you're going to kill us!

Aria   David was right – we're dead already.

She holds out her shard of glass as a warning for no one to follow them.

But I'd rather take my chances being dead out there.

We hear the door lock as she shuts the door to the sleeping area behind her.

Trevor   The emergency doors won't open! That was part of my script!

Peggy   They need to let us out – they can't let us die in here!

Trevor   Of course they will! That's why they sent me in here.

Aria *and* **Bella** *stack the mattresses up and set fire to the beds.*

Trevor (*shouting through the door of the sleeping area*)   The emergency doors won't open!

Bella (*from inside the sleeping area*)   I don't care what you say anymore!

Aria (*from inside the sleeping area*)   You've cried wolf too many times!

Layla *pushes* **Trevor** *out of the way and tries to pull the door open.*

Layla   Oh, for God's sake! What do you think you're doing?! Stop pouring gin on the mattresses! Idiots!

Peggy *is scared and goes over the table and picks up the long carving fork.*

Peggy   Hugo, how are you getting on?

Hugo   I'm trying! A couple more minutes maybe.

Peggy   Once those beds start to blaze, we'll only have minutes to get out.

Maddie   Cannae git it. A've tried aw the George Bernard Shaw dates A cin hink ae.

The room is filled with red flashing light. We hear the incinerator ignite and roar.

Trevor   If we can get into the Incinerator Room – there's a ventilation hatch in the ceiling. It leads up to the roof.

Maddie *tries another code. We hear a buzz, indicating it's wrong.*

Peggy We're gonna choke to death.

Trevor We need to get in there! Now!

Maddie A've tried iverythin A cin hink ae!

David Maybe there's another *Pygmalion* date we can try?

Layla What about the day George Bernard Shaw died?

Maddie Mynd that fae when A wis daen ma research. Second November – nineteen fifty. He died on ma sister's birthday.

She punches the numbers into the keypad.

Two, one, one, one, nine, five, zero. It's no workin!

Aria *and* **Bella** *are forced back into the main space by the roaring fire. Thick smoke follows them as they come back into the main space with a bottle of gin in one hand and their weapons in the other. They swig gin and cough as they enter the room.*

Layla What have you done!

Bella You'll thank us for it!

Aria *and* **Bella** *theatrically throw back their heads with their mouths open and tongues out, waiting for the sprinkler to come on. The room is now rapidly filling with smoke.*

Peggy Try it with a zero to start – zero two!

Maddie Zero, two, one, one, one, nine, five, zero.

We hear a buzz, indicating the code is wrong.

Peggy Can't breathe!

David *sticks the fish knife under* **Trevor**'s *chin.*

David (*to* **Trevor**)   Is there anything else it could be?

Trevor (*coughing*)   No, everything I was told was /

Peggy / What was the date?! World premiere of *Pygmalion*!

Layla Why would it be that?!

Peggy   YOU GOT ANY BETTER IDEAS!

Layla   It could be anything!

David   IT'S WORTH A TRY!

Maddie   Cannae mynd the date.

David   TRY TO REMEMBER!

Maddie   A DINNAE KEN IT!

David   It'll be in the play script!

He grabs the Pygmalion *script out of the rucksack and finds the date at the front of the text. As he shouts out the numbers* **Maddie** *punches them into the keypad.*

David   One! Six! One! Zero! One! Nine! One! One – no. Sorry. Three!

Maddie   Whit is it?! Wan ir three!

David   Three! Three – it's three.

There is a positive beep and **Maddie** *opens the door. They all hesitate. We hear a crackly and faint voice from the makeshift radio.*

Hugo   It's working!

Government Announcer   The new variant is spreading exponentially. Do not leave your homes. Do not go outside. This is paramount. Anyone seen outside will be shot on sight.

They look at each other for leadership but no one knows what to do. They are all petrified and sick with fear.

Blackout.

Printed in the USA
CPSIA information can be obtained
at www.ICGtesting.com
LVHW020934171024
794056LV00003B/763